PEACOCKS

LIVING WILD

Published by Creative Education and Creative Paperbacks
P.O. Box 227, Mankato, Minnesota 56002
Creative Education and Creative Paperbacks are imprints of The Creative Company
www.thecreativecompany.us

Design and production by Mary Herrmann
Art direction by Rita Marshall
Printed in China

Photographs by Creative Commons Wikimedia (The British Library, Adrian Collaert, The Edge Gallery, Frankyboy5, Gfmorin, Arjan Haverkamp, Dr. Raju Kasambe, Mitternacht90, Jurgen Otto, Quartl, Rama, Trisha Shears, Archibald Thorburn, Victoria and Albert Museum), Dreamstime (Manit Larpluechai), iStockphoto (AmazingDream, gui00878, IntergalacticDesignStudio, JenD, Enrique Ramos Lopez, SoumyaBalakrishnan, taeya18, YunYulia), Shutterstock (apiguide, Kitch Bain, marilyn barbone, Mikhail Blajenov, chanus, dangdumrong, Mila Drumeva, eska2005, Oleg Golovnev, kungverylucky, Lmnopg007, Chumash Maxim, nld, Tobie Oosthuizen, Matyas Rehak, Saranvaid, Roongroj Sookjai, SurangaSL, Brian Tan, Nikita Tiunov, Volga, Ashley Whitworth, YANGCHAO)

Library of Congress Cataloging-in-Publication Data
Gish, Melissa.
Peacocks / Melissa Gish.
p. cm. — (Living wild)
Includes bibliographical references and index.
Summary: A look at peacocks, including their habitats, physical characteristics such as the male's colorful plumage, behaviors, relationships with humans, and the protected status of Congo and green peacocks in the world today.

ISBN 978-1-60818-707-2 (hardcover)
ISBN 978-1-62832-303-0 (pbk)
ISBN 978-1-56660-743-8 (eBook)
1. Peafowl—Juvenile literature. I. Title. II. Series: Living wild.

QL696.G27G57 2016
598.6'258—dc23   2015026823

CCSS: RI.5.1, 2, 3, 8; RST.6-8.1, 2, 5, 6, 8; RH.6-8.3, 4, 5, 6, 7, 8

First Edition HC 9 8 7 6 5 4 3 2 1
First Edition PBK 9 8 7 6 5 4 3 2 1

CREATIVE EDUCATION • CREATIVE PAPERBACKS

PEACOCKS

Melissa Gish

In India's Mudumalai National Park, an Indian peacock roams the forest floor in search of fallen berries and seeds. The colorful bird holds his long tail feathers aloft.

In India's Mudumalai National Park, an Indian peacock roams the forest floor in search of fallen berries and seeds. The colorful bird holds his long tail feathers aloft. Suddenly, he hears a rustling in the brush and freezes in his tracks. He sees movement and immediately leaps into the air, flapping his broad wings. Landing on the lowest branch of a neem tree, above the reach of predators, the peacock sounds the alarm: *Ay-yow! Ay-yow! Ay-yow!* From his perch, the peacock waits and watches with a keen eye. But no predator steps out from the brush below. Instead, a potential mate approaches. She tilts her head and looks up at the male, who descends from the tree. He steps forward, bobbing his head. Then he lifts his tail, spreading his fabulous feathers. He plans to impress this female with a showy display.

WHERE IN THE WORLD THEY LIVE

■ **Indian Peacock**
India, Sri Lanka

■ **Java Peacock**
Myanmar to
Indonesia

■ **Congo Peacock**
Democratic Republic
of the Congo

The three species of richly colored peacocks are named for their native geographical locations. Indian and Java peafowl are found in Asia—Indian peafowl on the Indian subcontinent and Java peafowl in fragmented habitats from Myanmar to Indonesia. Congo peafowl are native to Central Africa, primarily the rainforests of the Democratic Republic of the Congo. The colored squares represent where each peacock species lives in the wild today.

eafowl are some of the most beautiful birds in the animal kingdom. Although, technically, only males are peacocks (females are peahens), "peacock" is the term commonly applied to all peafowl. The three peacock species are named for their places of origin: the Indian (or blue) peacock, the Java (or green) peacock, and the Congo peacock. The blue peacock became the national bird of India in 1963. The green peacock of Southeast Asia is an endangered species. Both birds are well known for their stunning blue and green **plumage**, which includes long, colorful tail feathers, called trains, displayed by males. The rare Congo peacock has colorful feathers but lacks a train. Found in the Democratic Republic of the Congo and called *mbulu* in Congolese, this peacock is the country's national bird.

Peacocks are members of the family Phasianidae (*FAY-zee-AH-nuh-day*), which also includes chickens, junglefowl, partridges, pheasants, and some species of quail. The family is named for the ancient city of Phasis and the Phasis River (now the Rioni River in the present-day country of Georgia). About 3,000 years ago,

Like their peafowl cousins, male and female pheasants have differences in tail length and feather coloration.

Peacocks were so admired by the Romans that the birds inspired pieces of jewelry such as this brooch.

Sri Lankans consider the courtship of blue peacocks to be a sign that **monsoon** season is close at hand.

the ancient Greeks introduced blue and green peacocks as well as various pheasant species to the Phasis region, calling them collectively "Phasian birds." Their beauty made them popular throughout the later Roman Empire. In the 11th century, Crusaders took the birds from the Black Sea region to Europe. Pheasants then became important game birds, while peacocks were raised to delight—and feed—the wealthy. By the 18th century, peacocks had spread around the world.

Today, wild peacocks still inhabit their native lands in India, Southeast Asia, and Central Africa. **Domesticated** peacocks can be found in parks and zoos and on farms on nearly every continent. In wilderness and urban areas alike, peacocks have escaped captivity and established **feral** flocks. Some American cities, including Los Angeles, Houston, and Miami, consider feral peacocks invasive pests. In the wild, peacocks are tropical birds that inhabit forests and rainforests. They typically feed on the ground and sleep in trees. They do not fly long distances in search of food or mates like many other birds do, and they do not **migrate**.

Like all birds, peacocks are warm-blooded, feathered, beaked animals that walk on two feet and lay eggs. Their

Domesticated blue peacocks are kept on estates and in parks around the world, adding exotic beauty to the locations.

In 2014, a Canadian study found that a male peacock's quivering tail feathers emit a low sound humans cannot hear.

mostly hollow bones make their bodies lightweight for easier flight. Male blue peacocks are the largest peacocks. They can have a wingspan stretching more than five feet (1.5 m). They weigh 9 to 13 pounds (4.1–5.9 kg), with a body length of 3 to 5 feet (0.9–1.5 m). The length of the male blue peacock's train can exceed five feet (1.5 m). Green and Congo peacocks are much smaller, weighing only about half as much as male blue peacocks. Female blue peacocks are typically six to nine pounds (2.7–4.1 kg), and their bodies are shorter than males'. Females of all species are smaller than males and lack trains. Such a difference in size and color between males and females is called sexual dimorphism.

The peacock's most striking feature is its plumage. Feathers grow individually, much like hairs grow on **mammals**. Soft and fluffy feathers, called down, help protect the peacock's body. Small, tightly spaced contour feathers cover the down. These feathers are **iridescent** and get their colors from biochromes, which are substances the body produces from chemical processes.

Male blue and green peacocks have a colorful feather crest on top of the head and long tail feathers (called covert feathers), which grow over the shorter contour feathers.

A peacock's feather crest is made up of threadlike, tufted feathers called filoplumes.

At the height of mating season, a mature peacock's train can have as many as 200 individual feathers.

San Diego Zoo researchers found that peacocks can make noise as loud as a police siren—up to 100 decibels.

Each of the tail feathers has a distinctive eye-like image called an ocellus (the plural of which is "ocelli"). Male Congo peacocks have a white crest and short tails. Peahens of all species are far less colorful than males. Their feathers and crests are mostly dull black, gray, or brown. While males use their vibrant feathers to attract mates, females rely on their drab feathers for **camouflage** when nesting and foraging with their offspring, called peachicks.

Peacocks have scaly legs. Their feet are anisodactyl, meaning three toes point forward and one toe points backward. Each toe ends in a sharp claw that is used to scrape the ground to stir up insects and grip branches while roosting in trees. Peacocks sleep in groups high off the ground to evade most predators. Their only defense against an attacker is to peck with their sharp beaks— which doesn't usually work against wild dogs or tigers. Rather than fight, peacocks prefer to run into dense underbrush and hide from danger. Although they are not strong fliers, they will take to the air if trapped.

Like other birds, peacocks rely on vision as their strongest sense. Peacocks have large eyes set on the sides of their head. This allows them to see both forward and

With heavy bodies and small wings, peacocks are incapable of flying long distances but will take flight to avoid predators.

Predators up above may not notice camouflaged peahens, but brightly colored males (pictured) may attract attention.

to the sides. Their eyes have a nictitating (*NIK-tih-tayt-ing*) membrane (a see-through inner eyelid) to help protect them from dust and debris. With four special cells called photoreceptors in each eye, birds can see ultraviolet light that humans and many other animals cannot see. This sharpens the images that peacocks see, so they can detect the slightest movement and react quickly to danger. Vision doesn't always save peacocks, though. They do not see well in the dark, so they are often attacked by leopards, mongooses, and eagles while roosting in trees at night.

Peacocks spend much of their day foraging for food. They mostly eat insects, seeds, leaves, berries, and flowers, but they may nab small lizards, frogs, and rodents when available. Peacocks also ingest grit and tiny pebbles to aid in digestion. Like most birds, peacocks have a multipart digestive system, beginning with a crop, which is located at the base of the neck. The crop stores food and releases it in small portions to the two-part stomach. The first part, called the proventriculus, contains digestive juices that break down food. The second part is the ventriculus, or gizzard, where ingested grit and stones grind food into liquid mush, making it easy to digest.

Green peacocks can be found in the dense bamboo forests of Sri Lanka.

A peacock's diet is made up of about 30 percent protein, which means that it eats a lot of insects.

If a predator grabs onto a male peacock's train, the feathers will easily come out, allowing the peacock to escape.

PECKING, PREENING, AND PARTIES

Peacocks in the wild typically live about 15 years, though well-fed birds kept safely in captivity can live to be 20 or 25. Peacocks reach maturity and are ready to mate between two and three years old. However, a male will not have a full train until he is three years old. Without a full train, he is unlikely to attract females, as peahens are most impressed by long trains featuring elaborate ocelli. Peacocks are polygynous, meaning they have more than one mating partner. To accomplish this, males gather several females together to form a harem.

During mating season, which extends from April into early August, mature males gather in a group called a lek. Within the lek, each bird participates in courtship rituals to attract mature females. They strut and dance around, squawking loudly to catch the females' attention. When a male has gathered an audience of peahens, he lifts his train, spreading it six to seven feet (1.8–2.1 m) wide, and vibrates his feathers. The shimmering, iridescent feathers mesmerize the peahens. If the male's train is impressive enough, four or five

Unlike albino animals, leucistic peacocks have the same eye color as normal peacocks.

Some peacocks are all-white because of a genetic condition called leucism, which causes their feathers to lack color.

Derived from the male peacock's elaborate courtship rituals, a group of peacocks is sometimes called an "ostentation."

peahens will approach him. This new group becomes the peacock's harem.

The male will mate with all the females in his harem. Afterward, he leaves the harem and plays no part in nesting or raising offspring. Near the end of summer, changes in his **hormones** signal a time for transformation: his tail feathers begin to fall out. This process, called molting, occurs in males every year after mating season. Feathers are made of keratin, the same substance found in human fingernails. Keratin cannot be replaced if damaged—it must be completely regrown. Just as humans clip broken fingernails, birds must drop their worn and damaged feathers and regrow new ones. In peacocks, the entire train falls out, and it takes about seven months to fully replace it. Each year until a peacock is six, its train grows back a little longer and fuller.

After mating, a peahen is ready to lay her first egg. She does this in an open space where it is exposed to other animals. The laying of this egg, called a decoy egg, is intended to attract the attention of potential predators, while the peahen heads in the opposite direction. The peahen may, in fact, lay several decoy eggs until she feels confident that she will be safe in making a nest. Finding a secluded spot under a bush or fallen tree, the peahen scratches a depression in the dirt. She may kick a few leaves into the depression. Here she lays four to six eggs at a rate of one egg per day. The ivory-colored eggs are more than twice the size of chicken eggs.

Like all birds' eggs, peacock eggs must be incubated, or kept warm, while the baby birds develop inside. Once all the eggs are laid, the peahen gently sits on the eggs situated under her breast and wings. Her body heat prompts the eggs to begin developing. She turns her eggs

Peahens that share nesting sites may warn each other of danger and thus better protect their eggs.

A 2014 Purdue University study suggested that a male's fancy footwork, not his feathers, might attract peahens.

Once male peachicks have developed covert tail feathers, they instinctively raise their tails when excited.

daily, which keeps the babies inside from sticking to one side of the inner shell. The peahen leaves once a day to eat, flying from the nest with loud squawks to lure any predators away from her hiding spot. Despite the peahen's vigilance, wild dogs, mongooses, snakes, and other birds may steal eggs or hatchlings. If this occurs in the spring, a peahen may mate again and lay more eggs. However, if she loses her babies during the summer, she will give up until the following year. The peahen incubates her eggs for about 28 days before the peachicks hatch.

A peachick begins to chirp inside its egg before hatching. Its mother chirps back. The hatchling chips through the hard shell with its egg tooth (the hard, toothlike tip of its beak used only for this purpose). Using its legs to push free of its shell, the little bird emerges wet, weak, and helpless. It takes about 12 hours for the fluffy down covering a peachick's body to dry. Within 24 hours of hatching, peachicks are able to walk and peck the ground for tiny bits of food. They follow their mother closely, and if danger approaches, they scurry under her wings for protection. Within two months, the peachicks' down is replaced by feathers that are the same color as

While adult peacocks can aggressively peck to fend off predators, peachicks have fewer defenses.

Similar to how chickens prefer a familiar evening roost, domesticated peacocks will stay close to the trees in which they sleep.

the peahen's. The peachicks can then follow their mother onto tree branches to sleep off the ground. Males develop their bright colors and grow their train as juveniles.

Peacocks are social birds that form groups called parties. They get along well with one another but not with other bird species. Peacocks communicate by using 11 different vocalizations, from alarming shrieks to mating cries. They typically follow a twice-daily routine of foraging, drinking water, preening (or grooming) their feathers, and resting or sleeping close together on tree branches. Like all birds, peacocks preen regularly to maintain their health. Preening is also vital to keeping feathers smooth and straight, which prevents breakage. Each feather on a peacock's body has a central shaft with two vanes extending from each side. Each vane is made up of a series of hundreds of slender branches called barbs. Further, each of these barbs is covered with even smaller branches called barbules. And each barbule has tiny hooks that fit together, giving a healthy feather the appearance of a solid surface. To keep all the barbules properly hooked together, a bird must preen.

Using its beak, a peacock removes dirt and **parasites** before pulling each feather through its beak in such a way as to hook all the barbules together. The bird also uses its beak and feet to cover its feathers with an oily substance produced by the uropygial gland, or preen gland, found near the base of the tail. This preen oil helps waterproof the feathers and keep them flexible. Because too much preen oil will weigh down the feathers, peacocks take dust baths. They use their feet and wings to kick up dust, which absorbs excess preen oil and dislodges parasites in the process.

The peacock's neck is thin and flexible, enabling the bird to reach all its feathers for preening.

Two peacock vocalizations, the mating cry and alarm shriek, can be heard as far away as five miles (8 km).

In the Christian tradition, the ocelli on a peacock's tail feathers became symbolic of God's all-seeing eyes.

BIRD OF IMMORTAL BEAUTY

or thousands of years, the peacock has appeared in stories and artwork, its beauty symbolizing everything from selfish vanity to noble devotion. The ancient Greeks included peacocks in the stories of their gods and goddesses. They believed these birds pulled the chariot of Hera, the goddess of the sky and stars. According to one **myth**, Hera's husband, Zeus, planned to have an affair with the beautiful Io. Hera commanded her servant Argus to guard Io. Argus watched Io with his 100 eyes, but Zeus had Argus killed. To reward her servant's sacrifice, Hera placed Argus's eyes on the tail of the peacock.

An ancient Greek book of **allegories** by an unknown author around A.D. 100 includes a story about the peacock's pride. According to the story, peacocks refuse to fly high because they do not want anyone to see their ugly, chicken-like feet. When a peacock catches a glimpse of its own feet, it is so horrified that it shrieks loudly. Such vanity prevents peacocks from escaping danger and instead often leads to their capture.

In ancient Chinese mythology, peacocks are thought of as compassionate and kind rather than proud. The

Peacock cichlids (SIK-lids) are colorful, iridescent fish native and restricted to Lake Malawi in East Africa.

The Hindu god Kartikeya, who is depicted as eternally young and beautiful, rides a blue peacock into battle.

birds have the power to grant protection. Quan Yin, the goddess of mercy, is often shown in artwork as being in the presence of peacocks. Her name means "one who hears the cries of others." In addition to helping people in danger, the goddess was believed to have the power of fertility. If a woman looked squarely at Quan Yin's peacock, the woman would become pregnant.

A folk tale from Laos paints a very different picture of the peacock, depicting this bird as jealous and spiteful. Long ago, the crow and peacock were best friends. In those days, both birds had plain white feathers. One day, while playing in a field of colorful wildflowers, the crow suggested that he and the peacock paint each other's feathers so that they, too, could be colorful. The peacock agreed, and the crow set to work painting fancy designs on his friend's feathers in the most stunning shades of blue, green, yellow, and orange. But the new feathers made peacock arrogant and jealous. He didn't want the crow to have prettier feathers than he, so the peacock poured black paint on the crow. This ended their friendship, and to this day, the crow caws grudgingly at the peacock, who arrogantly squawks back.

In A.D. 77, an account of peacocks appeared in the encyclopedia *Natural History,* written by Pliny the Elder, an ancient Roman naturalist and author. He described how the flesh of peacocks was so tough that it could not be cooked or consumed properly. He even suggested that peacock meat was too tough to decay. This was inaccurate, for peacock meat was a delicacy in the ancient world. Cleopatra, the queen of Egypt, as well as Alexander the Great and Roman senators all dined on peacocks.

Yet the peacock's reputation for having imperishable meat persisted. The early Catholics adopted the peacock as a symbol of resurrection and immortality. Images

Starting in the 11th century, peacocks were imported to northern European countries and then later depicted in art.

HOW THE PEACOCK GOT HIS BEAUTIFUL FEATHERS

When the world was young and when all the animals spoke the language of mankind, the peacock, U Klew, was but an ordinary grey-feathered bird without any pretensions to beauty. But, even in those days, he was much given to pride and vanity, and strutted about with all the majesty of royalty, just because his tuft was more erect than the tuft of other birds and because his tail was longer and was carried with more grace than the tails of any of his companions.

He was a very unaccommodating neighbour. His tail was so big and unwieldy that he could not enter the houses of the more lowly birds, so he always attended the courts of the great, and was entertained by one or other of the wealthy birds at times of festivals in the jungle. This increased his high opinion of himself and added to his self-importance. He became so haughty and overbearing that he was cordially disliked by his neighbours, who endeavoured to repay him by playing many a jest at his expense.

They used to flatter him, pretending that they held him in very high esteem, simply for the amusement of seeing him swelling his chest and hearing him boast. One day they pretended that a great Durbar of the birds had been held to select an ambassador to carry the greetings of the jungle birds to the beautiful maiden Ka Sngi, who ruled in the Blue Realm and poured her bright light so generously on their world, and that U Klew had been chosen for this great honour.

The peacock was very elated and became more swaggering than ever, and talked of his coming visit with great boastings, saying that not only was he going as the ambassador from the birds, but he was going in his own interests as well, and that he would woo and win the royal maiden for his wife and live with her in the Blue Realm.

The birds enjoyed much secret fun at his expense, none of them dreaming that he would be foolish enough to make the attempt to fly so far, for he was such a heavy-bodied bird and had never flown higher than a tree-top....

from Folk-Tales of the Khasis, *by Mrs. K. U. Rafy (c. 1920)*

of peacocks appear on the walls of the catacombs of St. Callixtus, Priscilla, and St. Sebastian in Rome (underground places used for Christian burials from about A.D. 150 to 410). The peacock symbolized the death of the mortal body and rebirth as a beautiful being in heaven. In the remains of the ancient city of Khersonesus (on the present-day Crimean Peninsula), a **mosaic** panel features a pair of peacocks standing before a vase. The birds represent Christians drinking from the waters of eternal salvation.

The peacock is also important in the religion of Islam. One story tells how the peacock sat in a tree and prayed for 70,000 years. Then God held up a mirror to the bird. The peacock was so grateful for its beauty that it laid itself down face-forward five times in reverence to God. This is how the Muslim ritual of praying five times a day came to be. In India, peacocks symbolize royalty and power. In the 17th century, the Peacock Throne was made for Shah Jahan, the emperor of India. Carved peacocks adorned the throne, which was coated in gold and embedded with jewels.

In modern times, the peacock is a popular animated character. In the world of manga, Coo is a peacock in *Yakitate!! Japan*, and Kuu is a peacock in *Katekyō Hitman*

Peacocks were among the plants and animals featured in the mosaic floor of an ancient church in Nahariya, Israel.

The Congo peacock was included in a set of North Korean stamps released in 1990 depicting various peacocks.

Reborn! Video game characters include Pavé, a peacock in Nintendo's *Animal Crossing* series, and Cyber Peacock, a robotic human-like peacock in Capcom's *Mega Man X4*. A ghostly white peacock named Lord Shen is featured in the 2011 DreamWorks movie *Kung Fu Panda 2*. Lord Shen plots to take over all of China. It is up to Po, the panda kung fu warrior, and his band of fighters to stop the evil bird.

Peacocks provide inspiration for a variety of creations, from fashion to paintings. The Swiss jeweler Chopard designed an $18,000 diamond-and-gold watch with a peacock on the face for its 2011 Animal World Collection. Fashion designers have created everything from hats and purses to capes and ballgowns featuring peacock feathers. Gianni Versace even designed a men's collection in iridescent peacock colors. The 17th-century Dutch artist Melchior d'Hondecoeter's six-foot-tall (1.8 m) portrait, *Peacocks*, hangs in New York City's Metropolitan Museum of Art. In 1875, American artist James McNeill Whistler painted an entire room with peacocks for an English patron. In 1919, the famous "Peacock Room" was dismantled and reassembled at the Freer Gallery of Art in Washington, D.C., where it can be seen today.

Postage stamps are a form of art that people called philatelists (*fil-AT-uh-lists*) study and collect, and peacock stamps are a favorite. These birds are featured on collectible stamp sets from Ceylon (1964), Burundi (1965), Dhufar (1973), Pakistan (1976), and Hungary (1977). In 2013, Taiwan released a souvenir stamp sheet commemorating 17th-century Chinese art featuring peacocks and other culturally important wildlife. The following year, the Central African Republic released a souvenir sheet with four peacocks in various poses. Such sheets include stamps as part of full-page artwork, and collectors often frame them like mini paintings.

Melchior d'Hondecoeter specialized in painting birds and featured peacocks in many of his works.

Green peacocks have yellow markings on their cheeks and straighter, narrower crest feathers than blue peacocks.

LOVED TO DEATH

For the most part, wild peacocks are under-researched and poorly understood. This makes them difficult to conserve as forests are converted to farmland or altered by the logging and mining industries. Peacocks can be elusive as well, making their capture for data collection exceedingly difficult. The blue peacock is not in danger, as this abundant species has a wide range, but its cousins are not so fortunate. Both the Congo and green peacock appear on the Red List of Threatened Species that is published annually by the International Union for Conservation of Nature (IUCN).

The exact population of Congo peacocks is unknown. The IUCN estimates that anywhere from 3,500 to 15,000 birds exist in Africa. The greatest threat to Congo peacocks is habitat loss. Logging and mining operations (as well as the roads and towns they create) destroy forests, poison the land, and force wildlife into contact with humans. Also, war and poverty in the lands of Congo peacocks have led many people to hunt and trap wildlife to survive. Not only are peacocks targeted by hunters, but they are also easily caught in traps intended for other animals. In addition,

Despite being shorter than other peacock species' tails, the male Congo peacock's tail feathers have eyespots.

A peacock does not know its own reflection and will attack it— which can lead to scratched cars and broken windows.

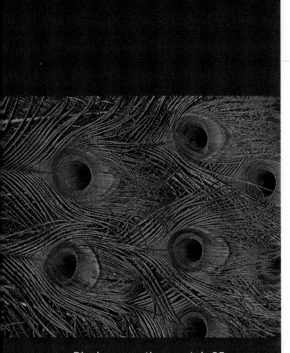

Biochromes—tiny crystals 25 times thinner than a human hair—are what make peacock feathers shimmer.

Despite the damage they cause to crops, peacocks are tolerated on farms in India because they kill snakes.

nesting females are killed and their eggs taken, which further contributes to the species' population decline. The IUCN has classified the Congo peacock as vulnerable, which means that if steps are not taken to protect this bird, it could face endangerment and eventual **extinction**.

The green peacock is in even graver danger than its African relative. Although between 15,000 and 30,000 green peacocks are believed to exist in the wild, their numbers are rapidly declining. Human actions are the number-one reason the IUCN has classified the green peacock as endangered. Habitat loss is the greatest threat to green peacocks. When the birds are pushed into living alongside humans, problems follow. Dr. Nicholas W. Brickle, an **ornithologist** at the University of Sussex, led two studies of green peacocks in central Vietnam. Over a period of 15 years, Brickle noted a steep decline in the population, determining in 2014 that waning access to water was partly to blame.

As human settlements expand, peacocks' habitats are affected. Pesticides used in agricultural practices may poison plants and water that peacocks need to survive. Despite peacocks' protected status in China, farmers in

that country consider green peacocks to be **nuisance** animals and routinely poison them. The birds are hunted and their eggs collected, while chicks are taken and sold by exotic animal dealers. And the demand for peacock tail feathers is so great that impatient traders will buy dead birds just to harvest their feathers.

Habitat **fragmentation** is also a problem. Too many birds in too small a space means too little food. Furthermore, when birds are confined to shrinking habitats, they are forced to mate with their relatives, which can lead to sickness and **genetic** disease. Green

The rachis is the thick, white stemlike structure that can be seen at the center of each tail feather.

The Congo peahen has a featherless throat that can be pink, red, or copper-colored, while the male's throat is a vivid red.

peacocks enjoy safety in protected areas such as the Huai Kha Khaeng Wildlife Sanctuary in Thailand and the Yok Don National Park in Vietnam. However, these birds have been eliminated from much of their former range, including northern India, Bangladesh, and Myanmar (Burma). Despite its status as the national bird of India, the blue peacock has no legal protection in that country.

One of the best hopes for Congo peacocks is **captive-breeding**. In 1959, two Congo peacocks were sent to the Antwerp Zoo in Belgium, where a captive-breeding program began. In 1971, the zoo established the Congo Peafowl Trust and committed to raising peafowl for distribution to zoos around the world. Unlike blue peacocks, which have been domesticated, Congo peacocks often get stressed and sick when taken out of their natural habitat. Captive-breeding these birds is extremely difficult. About 150 Congo peacocks live in captivity around the world today, and all of them are descendants of the first pair to live at the Antwerp Zoo. The zoo maintains a studbook, which is a way of tracking the family relationships of all the captive Congo peacocks in the world. Such records help ensure genetic diversity in the captive population by helping biologists determine which birds should breed with each other.

Organizations such as Indonesia's Friends of the National Parks Foundation (FNPF) rescue, rehabilitate, and release green peacocks that are injured or made ill by human activities. The birds include victims of accidental poisoning, animal attacks, and auto collisions. Birds that are trapped and caged for illegal sale at exotic animal markets are sometimes rescued as well. The goal of rescue centers is to help the peacocks return to the wild. In

The peacock spider of Australia dances and raises a colorful tail fan to impress females during courtship.

When previously domesticated peacocks escape their owners, they become feral, or instinctively wild.

2013, after nearly a year of healthcare and rehabilitation, five green peacocks were released into Alas Purwo National Park on the island of Java. Such actions are small but important measures in the conservation of the species.

Blue peacocks are naturally calmer than their Congo and green cousins, so they have become popular on poultry farms around the world. They first arrived in the United States in 1879 and quickly spread across the country, viewed more as novelties than farm animals. While peacock farms in North America exist mostly as a means of collecting feathers, farms in China raise peacocks for meat. Peacocks are typically roasted and taste like pheasants, quail, and other ground-dwelling game birds. In the southern U.S., feral populations of blue peacocks have become nuisance animals.

In 1936, several birds escaped from an estate in southern California. They took up residence in Angeles National Forest and began reproducing. Since then, nearby Gould Canyon, a neighborhood on the edge of Los Angeles, has come to be known as Peacock Alley because hundreds of peacocks inhabiting the forest now frequent the suburb. While many people admire the

grace and beauty of the birds, others hate the squawking, defecating, plant-eating pests. Gould Canyon is just one of many such urban areas overrun with feral peacocks.

While there may be only about 10,000 blue peacocks in the wild, these birds exist by the millions on farms and in zoos around the world. Congo and green peacocks are the species that have natural resource specialists most concerned. Global efforts to conserve peacocks must address challenging issues such as habitat loss, the exotic bird trade, and human interference. Without serious conservation measures implemented in their native lands, some peacock species may disappear from the planet altogether.

To remain healthy, domestic peacocks cannot be penned like chickens; they must be allowed to roam free.

ANIMAL TALE: THE PEACOCK AND THE JACKAL

Peacocks have long appeared in Islamic religious stories of the Middle East. One of the greatest storytellers in the Muslim tradition was Jalal ad-Din Muhammad Rumi, who lived in 13th-century Persia (present-day Iran). According to the Koran, the holy book of Islam, Allah (or God) sees the actions of every living thing and places these beings into two categories: bad or good. *Sijjin* is the name of bad, and *Illiyyin* is the name of good. One of Rumi's stories tells how the peacock and the jackal came to symbolize *Illiyyin* and *Sijjin*.

One day, the jackal was scratching fleas out of his raggedy fur when he saw the peacock walk past. The bird held its tail high, and its magnificent plumage shimmered in the sun. The jackal sat motionless and watched the fantastically colored bird. He felt great envy, wishing his coat had the bright colors of the peacock. "Why can't I be beautiful?" the jackal grumbled. "I hate being ugly."

The peacock heard the jackal and stopped to say, "Dear jackal, nothing that Allah has made in the world is ugly. He sees beauty in every living thing."

"Oh, just leave me alone," muttered the jackal, loping away.

Later in the day, the jackal came upon a group of women dyeing hijabs, or Muslim scarves, in great vats of colorful dye. The jackal thought he could change the way Allah had made him, so he slipped silently into one of the vats and sat there for a long time. Then he crept into another vat, and then another and another until his fur was dyed many different colors. The jackal was thrilled and raced home to show off his new look.

When he reached the other jackals, they all looked at him in disbelief. "You crazy jackal," they cried. "Why would you do such a thing?"

"Excuse me?" the jackal said innocently. "I am no jackal. I am a peacock. Behold my beautiful colors."

"You should not tell lies," the other jackals said.

"I am not lying," the jackal insisted. "I am not an ugly jackal. I am a beautiful peacock."

"You should not say that anything Allah has made is ugly," the other jackals cautioned.

They ran to fetch the peacock. "He is disrespecting Allah by pretending to be something he is not," they told the peacock. "You must help him mend his mistake."

The peacock ruffled his feathers and lifted his tail so that the sun shimmered on his body. "Can you do this?" he asked the jackal.

The jackal fluffed his fur and raised his tail. The sun shimmered on his dyed fur.

"All right," the peacock continued, "can you do this?" Then he cried out with a distinctive peacock call.

The jackal cried out in his very best imitation of a peacock call.

"Very good," the peacock said, "but can you do this?" He flapped his wings, lifted himself off the ground, and flew in a circle around the jackals.

Alas, the colored jackal could not fly. He was forced to admit his fraud. For his deceit, Allah made the jackal a symbol of *Sijjin.* For his compassion in trying to help the jackal admit his mistake, Allah made the peacock a symbol of *Illiyyin*.

GLOSSARY

allegories – stories, poems, or pictures that can be interpreted to reveal hidden meanings or morals

camouflage – the ability to hide, due to coloring or markings that blend in with a given environment

captive-breeding – being bred and raised in a place from which escape is not possible

domesticated – tamed to be kept as a pet or used as a work animal

extinction – the act or process of becoming extinct; coming to an end or dying out

feral – in a wild state after having been domesticated

fragmentation – the breaking up of an organism's habitat into scattered sections that may result in difficulty moving safely from one place to another

genetic – relating to genes, the basic physical units of heredity

hormones – chemical substances produced in the body that control and regulate the activity of certain cells and organs

iridescent – showing shimmering colors that seem to change when viewed from different angles

mammals – warm-blooded animals that have a backbone and hair or fur, give birth to live young, and produce milk to feed their young

migrate – to undertake a regular, seasonal journey from one place to another and then back again

monsoon – a seasonal wind that brings rain in Southeast Asia and India

mosaic – a picture or design made by arranging small pieces of colored material such as glass, stone, or tile

myth – a popular, traditional belief or story that explains how something came to be or that is associated with a person or object

nuisance – something annoying or harmful to people or the land

ornithologist – a scientist who studies birds and their lives

parasites – animals or plants that live on or inside another living thing (called a host) while giving nothing back to the host; some parasites cause disease or even death

plumage – the entire feathery covering of a bird

SELECTED BIBLIOGRAPHY

Fowler, Erin. "*Pavo cristatus*." Animal Diversity Web. http://animaldiversity.ummz.umich.edu/accounts /Pavo_cristatus.

Heinrichs, Christine. *How to Raise Poultry: Everything You Need to Know*. Minneapolis: Voyageur Press, 2014.

Jackson, Christine E. *Peacock*. London: Reaktion Books, 2006.

National Geographic. "Peacock." http://animals .nationalgeographic.com/animals/birds/peacock.

Roberts, Michael. *Peacocks: Past and Present*. Norfolk, U.K.: Gold Cockerel Books, 2003.

Smithsonian National Zoological Park. "Meet Our Animals: Indian Peafowl." http://nationalzoo.si.edu /Animals/Birds/Facts/fact-peafowl.cfm.

Although native to only India, blue peacocks now add beauty and wonder to many parks and preserves worldwide.

INDEX